The Sandcastle Diary

Louis-Philippe Hébert

BookLand press

Published by BookLand Press
15 Allstate Parkway, Suite 600, Markham, Ontario L3R 5B4
www.booklandpress.com

Printed and bound in Canada

Front cover image © Katrina Brown | Dreamstime.com

Library and Archives Canada Cataloguing in Publication

Hébert, Louis-Philippe, 1946-, author
The sandcastle diary / Louis-Philippe Hébert

Poems.
Issued in print and electronic formats.
ISBN 978-1-926956-74-9 (pbk.).--ISBN 978-1-926956-75-6 (epub).--
ISBN 978-1-926956-76-3 (pdf)

I. Title.

PS8515.E2S25 2014	C811'.54	C2013-907072-9
		C2013-907073-7

Canada Council for the Arts Conseil des arts du Canada

ONTARIO ARTS COUNCIL
CONSEIL DES ARTS DE L'ONTARIO
50 YEARS OF ONTARIO GOVERNMENT SUPPORT OF THE ARTS
50 ANS DE SOUTIEN DU GOUVERNEMENT DE L'ONTARIO AUX ARTS

We acknowledge the support of the Canada Council for the Arts, which last year invested $157 million to bring the arts to Canadians throughout the country. We acknowledge the support of the Ontario Arts Council (OAC), an agency of the Government of Ontario, which last year funded 1,681 individual artists and 1,125 organizations in 216 communities across Ontario for a total of $52.8 million. We acknowledge the financial support of the Ontario Media Development Corporation for our publishing activities.

For Ardeth, Suzanne, Genevieve and
many other women on the beach that day
when the sun was high and the tide was low

Table of Contents

CHAPTER ONE
Killing Zombies

I shouldn't have come here
in the first place
that was the only thing you said
for a whole week
you looked at the sea
you looked at the beach
and then you looked at the sun
longer than I thought it was possible for anyone to do
and then
out of the blue
you said
I shouldn't have come to this place
you paused
it will give you bad memories

you considered the whole thing
I think, what was happening to you
the sickness
more than the sickness, the process
as you called it
the therapy
what you will have to go through
and you completed the sentence
I shouldn't be
you said
here
I shouldn't be here

why don't you go outside and play
with the other kids?
normally, that would have brought a smile
not tears
the mother and the boy
the mother doing mother's work
the kid playing a game of shoot'em up
I'm killing zombies, mommy
I can't go right now
I'm killing zombies
before they invade us

even that reply didn't make you laugh
you didn't want to talk
it was your grandson
you didn't want to think
you had your shoes on
you didn't feel the sand
so warm
so hot it burned
burning sand from a hot day
on the beach

I was wandering around you
like those little dogs
running around their master
but I did everything I could
so it wouldn't be noticeable
I was just trying to get you moving
and then, to keep you on the move

I did the work mentally
and physically
look at me, look at me
say something
I ended up with both feet in the sea
sure, the water was cold
I was freezing
you were not looking

you didn't seem to bother
the tide could have taken me
you were somewhere else
the doctor had told you
now is the time for you to do
            whatever you really wanted to do
you looked at him
maybe in the same way you were looking at me now
and said
kill myself

it was not an option
but we discussed it
we negotiated
it was a strange kind of a negotiation
we decided to go to the beach house
and you had no objections
you said to me
let's go
I think these were the last words I've heard from you
let's go

so, let's go
let's go, let's take a walk
maybe we will see a sea urchin
find a baby crab
come on, we will find a shell
a special one, something, anything

I will give you a dollar for every sand dollar
you bring back
she is your daughter
don't look at me like that
she was not being helpful, I know
while I was trying to be
speak softly
she was shouting at him
go outside, come on, get out of the house
and the boy
I am killing zombies
I am killing zombies, mommy
I can't stop
they are spreading everywhere
put it on pause

I could see your eyes behind your sunglasses
and I was sure you were going to say something
but you didn't
your eyes
I will always remember your eyes
that's the kind of thing nobody wants to hear about
I don't talk about it normally

but tonight
I am killing zombies

CHAPTER TWO
What Will Happen If You Die?

Today
I think that from now on
all my diary's days
will begin with today
is there anything else?
who needs to know if it's Monday
today
the third or the fifth
of January
the sun is so bright
it could be August

you were sleeping
I think
I think you were sleeping
your eyes were closed
you were breathing normally
I mean with a certain kind of regularity
which is yours when you are sleeping
but you haven't had a lot of sleep lately

you had your hands crossed behind your head
and, for a moment
I thought of pulling down the sheets
to have a complete view of your naked body
without you knowing it
without that kind of shyness
or that kind of vanity

aren't they the same?
the way someone acts
when somebody else is looking at him
you, men, are always trying to hide
or to show yourself
aren't you?

when we were a bit younger
you were acting out in front of me
with that kind of self-assurance
that made me think
about the elegance of an actor showing off
for an actress

that is the way you used to sell insurance
it would have been too easy to scare people
            by telling them a horrible story
like what will happen if you die, Honey?
and you, sir, who would take care of the baby?
no, that was not your style
you preferred to be moving around them
like in a dance

how do I know?
you used the same method to seduce me
using your body more than your mind
making the most subtle movements
something unforgettable
not a word uttered or whispered
nothing, not even a sound
not a squeak under your feet
and, finally, a pen ends up
by magic in the client's hand
where do I sign?

I can't insure you against nothing, you would say
some people would try to correct you
you mean the contrary
you can insure us against anything, can you?
a smile was your only answer
you always kept a low profile
were do I sign?

nothing aggressive would come out of you
smooth talker
you were the patient kind
no rush, we have all the time
they would thank you
thank you so much
and when we happened to run into them
    at the Hannaford
they would say oh hello, how are you?
they would seem concerned about your health
how could they know?
they were guessing, I suppose

so, these were the seven years of fat cows
like in the Bible, you know
we were piling up money
all in cash
nickels, dimes, quarters
and dollar bills
you had no confidence in banks
and we were looking at every real estate flyer
free magazines, ads from the agents
and guided tours on the Coldwell websites

I remember your fingers on the keyboard
the way you wrote numbers on paper
you softly drumming on the desk when it was
too slow
that very strange way you had of combing your
hair in the back
every small movement of yours was a dance

so I wondered this morning
today, today
is there any other day?
every day, from now on, will be today
I swear it

when you woke up, you were feeling better
you said: I feel fine
I feel like a million bucks
and you went out to the beach
with the kid
hey, come on, young man
he looked at you
let's go
he was a bit surprised
not more than me
he missed a few targets
game over, ok, I'll go with you
grandpa

I kept watching you from the porch
you dug a long, rectangular, hole in the sand
I was afraid it was too much effort
it would make you sweat
and that too much sun

would affect you badly
but you kept working at that hole
with all the magic that you used on me and
        your clients
and, after a few short minutes, you were done
there it was
a very neat hole in the ground
and a lot of kids were around
yelling go in it, go in it!

that's what you did
you didn't care about your jeans or your clean t-shirt
you just slipped down into the hole
falling gracefully
gracefully, that was the word I was searching for
and the kids
with their hands
had fun filling the hole
pushing the sand all over your body
not in my face, kids!
until there was only your head
out of the ground

how can I be so stupid?
I was thinking about the insurance
grandpa is dead, grandpa is dead!
kids will always be kids

CHAPTER THREE
Elisabeth With An "S"

I received the papers from the Police
about the car accident
they spelled my name with a *z*
can you imagine, they have it wrong again
will I have to go to the office personally?
every time I fill out the forms on the internet
the spell-checker bounces back with a *z*

you should definitely change it to a *z*
it would be easier for everybody
why all the fuss for an *s*
you tell me

it is my name, George
I'm French
that's the way they spell Elizabeth in France

Liz would be nice
nice and easy, if you want to know
and there wouldn't be any problems anymore

I can't, George

in the old days we could have talked like that for hours
it was not really an argument
I know, it doesn't sound that way
but George was kind of cool about it
the tone of his voice was smooth

he never tried to force me to do anything
it was only a suggestion on his part
he was always looking for an easy way
and, I think
I, his wife, was the most complicated thing in his life

I thought so until the death of Steve Birdsky
but that is another story
or is it really?
I shall keep it for a rainy day
with thunder and lightning

that day, I was only hoping that
our conversation would last
I would never say
that he was making a fuss about it, about my *s* or my *z*
that our conversation could last forever
was my only wish

George was talking
for the first time since we arrived at the beach
making complete sentences
yes, for the first time since our arrival three days ago

I think that George had been disturbed, even shocked
by the sight of the ocean
so far away from the protocol
his cancer
I don't know why we say the protocol
as if we were considering his cancer
a VIP guest in our life
a visitor from elsewhere that was always sitting
between us
taking the best seat in the room

he didn't dare to talk
George, I mean George
he would wander around the place
pacing like a dog who smells the presence of an
    unseen person
trying the kitchen cupboards
the broom cabinet
anywhere
pinching his nose
making a face that means do you smell it?
me shaking my head
no George
understood without a word

so here I was
with the man of a few words
on Route One
driving around, going to Rite Way and to Hannaford
and then to Wine and Cheese
all around Ogunquit
looking for groceries and pills
and a little bottle of French wine for me
don't forget Archie for the boy

he overheard
I don't want Archie
it's kiddie stuff
Samantha said
then buy it for me
she is still a young girl
our daughter is still a baby

with all the stop and go
reduced speed ahead signs
no turn on red
the green lights turning yellow
the car in front of us not knowing if it will go
or stop dead
and the sun kind of pushing heavily on the windshield
I would have thought
that George would remain silent
for a while
not at all

change it to Liz
that would be nice

I don't like it
I'm French, George
in French, it sounds like Lise
and I am not a Lise

well, you're not French either
you're an American
and, truly, you were never really French
you were a Canadian

a French Canadian, George
my parents spoke French
you used to say that you liked my accent

the funny accent
that's what I used to say
I like your funny accent

so you will have to live with the *s*
George, I'm an Elisabeth with an *s*
I am French

I have been told that it is mostly a dialect
nothing more
once you told me
they gave you that name Elizabeth
because of the Queen
can you imagine?
in honour of those who tried to eliminate your people
and us at one point
by the way

George, you're talking too much
you know it hurts
don't, please don't
let's change the subject

I will get better
and we will go to New Orleans
I'll show you around
you will see what happened to your ancestors
and
you will put a *z* in place of an *s*

we would never go there
George knew it, I think
he knew about the protocol
the stranger sitting at our table
or in the car between us
and New Orleans got struck
by a devastating hurricane

when he was in the hospital
I could see him trembling
when he watched the flood on TV
we won't go, Liz
you don't have to change your name anymore
you know

how could I contradict him?
these were his last days
he was driving with such care
being so intense
looking so deeply at the road
I had that secret wish
that we would have an accident

my husband is sick
Elisabeth, yes
it is spelled with an *s*, officer
my husband is sick, you know
and I am a French Canadian

CHAPTER FOUR
Silly Elisabeth

Sometimes, I imagine how you are
I try to compare
the way you are now
and the way you were then

it's silly, I know
but I see you in the grave
with all your beautiful clothes
the blazer, the grey pants
the extravagant tie with the baby angels
you used to say
it's a conversation piece
my clients like to comment on the tie
it keeps their mind away from the reality of life
remember, you bought the jacket
for Samantha's wedding
the wedding that never was

I look at the last picture they took of you
the one they gave to everybody at the funeral parlour
you in the coffin
with the puffy silky fabrics all around your body
and I try to see you in my mind
the way you are now
I mean rotten and everything

this is so silly
I'm a bit silly, you know it
and, guess what
I'm writing this page in the diary
with the pen you gave me for my 50th birthday
it's a fountain pen
these words are only enough to put me in a
        special mood
I feel even stranger when I think about it in French
"plume fontaine"
you know, like the fountain in Rome

I was so surprised when you explained to me
that it was always the same water
that kept on feeding the flow
I was naive and so delighted
the water was spraying on the surface
of the small round pond
and on my face
I was shivering
was it love or was it the mist?

is it true, George
or is it one of your jokes?
no, you said
it's not a joke
that's the way it works
how can you believe
it's always fresh water
sometimes, I have trouble with the way you think

so, it was my 50th birthday
you gave me the pen
remember, I told you
my God, we are old, George
you said
it's a Waterman
it will last forever
when I called it a "plume fontaine"
you started laughing

I liked it so much when you laughed, George
you will be able to write
your silly poetry
even when I'm gone
yes, I know how silly my poems can be
like when I am trying to describe you
fully dressed
in your beautiful suit
and then
devoured by the ground
eaten down to the bones
the suit decaying over and around you
and everything
even the maggots
feeding on you

oh my God, George
I screamed when I saw the pen
it is so nice
and useful, you added

so I kept on writing
I never wrote with another pen
I write things like
Dear Diary, you know
Dear Diary, I am here to tell you how George was
the kind of humour
he had
and that special look that characterized him
a neat guy
a guy you can have confidence in
a guy who could sell you insurance for your dog
you said we could start a company
selling pet's life insurance
you started filling the paperwork
I was supposed to be a vice-president
but you've never filed them
I will do it later, you told me
but nothing lasts, George

you were sick already
I mean at that time
but it didn't show
eaten alive
I feel that I am being eaten alive
like in your silly poems

write something funny, for God's sake
just for once, please
about what?
about Joe The Carpenter, for instance
he is funny!

I never did
things got worse too fast
it slipped my mind

until this morning, dear diary
when Joe was at the cottage
looking around the house
before winter
I think he was searching for small jobs he could do

and you know what he did, George?
he went on talking and talking
he talks a lot, you used to say

he told me that this kitchen window
on the sea side
is badly damaged
the sill is totally gone, he said
I said
Joe Smallwood, he goes by that name now
it's written in bold letters on his truck
Joe, don't try to get me into repairs I cannot afford
your husband would have liked it top shape
it's a beach house, Joe Smallwood
the sill seems ok to me
no, Dear, it's not
the paint covers everything
but inside it is completely rotten
and he took his screwdriver
and he just went on with it
I couldn't stop him from doing it
he pushed on the sill with the screwdriver
like somebody plunging a knife

into a body
there was nothing to resist the blade
the screwdriver went directly into the sill
up to the handle

you see, Dear
you see what I mean?
the outside is good
the inside is bad

I thought so
you know what?
when he pulled out his screwdriver
I was expecting blood
to flow out of the hole
and how happy I was that it did not

I'm silly
and it's getting worse
since you died, George

nice pen you've got there, Dear
Joe Smallwood said
I'll start on Monday
I'll need an advance for the materials
very nice pen
I was writing the check
thanks, it was from George, I answered
and I started crying

silly me!

CHAPTER FIVE
Lovely Day, Isn't It, Ladies

They were talking, George
they were simply talking
talking silly talk
I don't know why they got on your nerves
they smell
the reason is they smell
oh! George!
don't say that
I can smell them from here
perfumes, expensive sunscreens, deodorants
what else?
we are on a beach, aren't we

why don't you take a walk
it's a low tide
you could dip your toes in the water
just take it easy
don't listen to them
we did everything to get here
the cottage
the sun
the sand and the sea
George, George, you're not listening to me

George got up
and he went to them
two old ladies
well, not that old

let say middle aged
talking their troubles away
trying to make sense
about their kids
who are not kids anymore
who are having kids of their own
and don't need any advice from anybody

nothing is right
one would say
my mother, you know
we decided we would go to Canada
did you?
we did
wine is so expensive in Montreal
not like in California
and everybody seems so lazy
nothing more to say
the food, the road
and young girls everywhere
dressed in such a way
you could expect the worst
my mother is not feeling well
not recognizing me in the morning
no
yes
asking me, who are you young lady
my God
can you imagine

I could hear them too
still, I had to listen carefully
nothing funny

but George had been standing
for a while
it was a small talk
I couldn't imagine why George was so interested
I stopped paying attention
I laid down on my beach towel
my tummy feeling the sand
through the fabrics
warm and snug
like a man holding me
and George so far away from me
as I could feel myself floating away
from the beach

.

so let me say, I was surprised
to hear coming from that far
I mean from under the other umbrella
lovely day, ladies, isn't it
but that was not all
and George was adding
have you ever noticed
that we don't see any young people around
here anymore
they shrugged
I could feel them from where I was
my head lifted
tilted in their direction
my umbrella started to bend under the wind
and I felt, for the first time, I think
the hot wind wrapping around me
the same way an undertow wave
can sweep you away
from your life

CHAPTER SIX
Little Indian Chief Sleeping Pill

Look at the boy
look how he sleeps
don't disturb him, George

oh, George
you took Samantha by the arm
and you said in a low quiet voice
he looks like an Indian
those thick black hair
or something else
the nose
I don't know, Sam
maybe the way his legs are folded

look, he's dancing a rain dance now
see how his legs move
like they were stomping on the ground

the boy was sleeping on the couch
the boy's pyjama
a bit dropped down
showing a part of his little bum
cute
me behind Sam
saying cute
Sam behind her father
not saying anything

Sam, look
he is talking in his dream
he is asking something
can you hear him
what is he talking about
for God's sake

let him sleep, leave him alone
don't mess around with him
he has not slept like that for a long time
you know
first year of school
has been hard for him

but George, you couldn't help it
you couldn't take your eyes
off him
and you were so nervous
looking at him
examining every part
of the poor boy's body

his toes, look at the toes
they seem to be gripping on something
oh, his skin is so reddish
it's a sunburn line, dad
between where the bathing suit begins
and the t-shirt ends

and look, look, he is trying to smell
maybe it's
the smell of coffee brewing
look how his nostrils move
my God, it is strange
sleep is stranger than death
isn't it?
pa, don't talk about that

come on, George
have another coffee
and go sit in your chair
near the window
look at the beach
do something else
let the poor kid sleep

thanks
ok, I'm going
I'll sit here
and look
at the parking lot

don't be mad
it's just that we don't want you
to wake him up

Chief Sleeping Pill, huh?
I wonder who his father is

CHAPTER SEVEN
A Few Of Us

A few of us had the opportunity to enjoy
his loving manners
did I ever tell you so
nothing is easy with George
you never know how he is going to wake up

nothing is good enough for him
he hates the rain
he hates it when there is too much sun

here at the cottage
nothing is fitted for him
he is too tall for the ceiling
and he looks like a giant in the hide-a-bed

low tide, high tide
not enough or too many
it's like that suit we looked at
in the Ralph Lauren outlet
why do they make the sleeves so long
why three buttons
why that color
different from the one
that looks so good for the pants

the music is killing me
where is the guy for the fitting room
why do they lock it
for heaven's sake
I am not going to steal a pair of pants at my age

he would go on like that for hours
even in the car
but never one word louder than another
harsh realities being said so quietly
they sounded like a prayer

I think he is like that with us
so critical
because of his work
always looking for something new to satisfy a client
a new policy from Allstate
a new twist in life insurance
he would sit down and explain every word
with such calm

he would practice his speech with me
but I know him
George is someone special
black or white
heads or tails
depending how the nickel falls

you see what I am talking about
no, not exactly

staying at home would give him no satisfaction
he would always prefer to work
because work
particularly his kind of work
would bring him
into other people's homes
I think he wanted to know
how people lived
their joys, their sorrows
making him realize
that he could not be
someone else
or would not even want to be

that was the root of the problem
I believe
the origin of that strange sickness
being so unhappy
so deeply sad
knowing there was no escape for him
except in his head

that's how he started
playing the clown
in the circus of life

a few of us are really happy, you know
who lives a life without torments
tell me

I could hear him on the phone
even during the weekend
even at the beach
always sweet with his manners
always smooth talking
at first, I thought that all he wanted
was to know how people lived
their natural philosophy
that was his expression for it

Honey, happiness is a state of mind
don't let yourself slide
down the slippery slope
of depression
hang on
sooner or later, everything will look better

Honey, I offered you a good deal
it's up to you to sign it
no pressure
on anybody
your husband is sick
he won't last forever
you know that
I know that

the tone of his voice was subtle:
he's sick but the company doesn't know
so why don't we just do it now
sign it, send it back to me
or, no, better than that
I will pick up the papers at your house
tomorrow if you wish

so smooth
ok, I'll go
I'll be right at your house at eight

ending up the conversation
putting the phone down
or flipping closed the flip phone
no rush
ending up saying to me
with a snarl
crazy bitch

CHAPTER EIGHT
Oh My God, George, Oh My God

Let's go to the beach, Grandpa
please, oh, please
it's too hot, young man
it's too hot, isn't it, Sam

yes, the sun is very hot, darling
it's a scorcher

no way we're going to the beach
on a day like today

then, I want to go to Old Orchard
I want to go to the amusement park
mother

no, Junior, no, you won't go
it will be worse than the beach

Ma, I want to go

why don't you tell him a story, Dad

come over here, young man
I will tell you a very spooky tale

oh, yes, Grandpa

well, it was on a day like this
the temperature outside was 110 degrees
so hot, the water in the sea seemed to be boiling

George, what kind of story is that
you are scaring the kid

the boy was listening
eyes wide open, mouth too
everybody felt sleepy

you know, Junior, like in Africa
where they never work
even half a day like we do
because of the temperature
and they become lazy

Elisabeth scuffled
George, what are you getting at
and then, it was noon
the sun was at its peak
so I went to hide under the umbrella
it was so hot that day
I didn't want to walk to the parking lot
burn my feet walking on the sand
and then get in the car
turn the key
and be cooked like a turkey in the oven
before the air conditioning could start blowing
something else than stale air
that smells like a bad breath
you see, Junior
there was no escape for me

Mom, I'm scared

listen to Grandpa
Pa, stop being so descriptive
go to the facts

well, if you want to know
the fact is
that under such heat
I could hardly stay awake anymore
the sun, the wind
like a hair dryer blowing at full speed
and your grandmother was already sleeping
right beside me
under the umbrella
I felt dizzy

Ma, I'm so scared

get to the point, George
for God's sake

well, son, I fell asleep
on the beach towel
because the sun was moving
my head got under the sun's rays
and I slept so deep

while I was asleep
a very, very small crab
came from under the sand
searching for food
I didn't notice it
and it crawled over my face

is it possible, Mom
could this really happen, Grandma

Junior, listen to me
listen to the end of the story
the very small crab went down into my ear
it got inside the tube
which is called, as you remember from school,
    the Eustachian tube
and from there
you know what it did
it was hungry
the crab started digging and digging
for food
it could feel that at the end of the tunnel
there was my brain
tasty, oh, so tasty
boiling like a clam chowder for lunch
so it kept digging its way through
and it managed to get inside of my head
and it found the place comfortable
so it settled in there
you know what
it is still there

Ma
George

you see what it's doing
it's eating the brain

George, you are scaring him

not only that
you know what
crabs are born from little eggs
like chickens
yes, like chickens
so they are laying eggs
everywhere they can
and, when they are ready for it
all the baby crabs will hatch out of the shells
and they will eat me up
to the last bone
in my body

at that moment, George got up
he jumped like a madman
and with his two hands
thrown in front of him
snapping in the air
like claws
he reached for the boy

Junior stood up, crying
ah, don't be a crybaby
and the boy puked
vomiting all his food in front of him

oh, my God, George, oh, my God
look at the boy's face
he is so pale
George, don't move
you will spill everything on the floor

I am so scared, Mom
don't be afraid, Junior
Mom
George, for God's sake

your grandpa has a big problem in his head
what is it
a brain tumour, it's called a brain tumour

Grandpa, can the crab jump on me
for real?

CHAPTER NINE
Look! It's Me!

I'm there
with my funny dress
and there he is
can you see him in the picture
in the back
right behind me
oh, it was taken a few years ago
not long before we learned about the sickness
you know

can you make it bigger
Charlotte
look how pale he is already
and those strange eyes
what is he looking at
what is he watching
make it bigger once more
he looks so
desperate
maybe he knew already

and here
on the right
beside him
in the picture
it is Sam, Samantha
my daughter
isn't she lovely

she was always wandering around
when the picture was taken
going from one place to another
at that time
one boyfriend did lead to the next
she was so pretty
look at her face
she seems so tense
I know what was her concern
Junior would arrive five months later

next, please

and here he is
here is Junior
he is about five in that picture
going to school
his first year
yes, must have been five
he is so brilliant
first grade
first real contact with the rest of the humanity
or what's left of it
like George used to say
first glimpse at the atrocity of the world
George would add

come on, Pa
don't say that
look at her mouth
pouting

that is Sam
that is my baby
always fighting with her father
you can hear her if you want
I had the record button on

yes, Charlotte

just sit down
look and listen
that's life
life is
like a railroad crossing
better be careful
one train may hide another
I know that

next, please

look at Junior, now
he is at the beach
making a sandcastle
he feels so happy
you see
he is building something
on a sunny day like that
life can be wonderful
too bad George is not here anymore

to enjoy it
yes, to enjoy it

with me

point the arrow to the next one, dear
click on the next picture
come on darling
please go to the next one

unless
I don't know
there is nothing left to look at

CHAPTER TEN
You're Rich Now

So life went on
George was always nervous about everything
I used to take long walks along the sea to think
I have the impression that it was the only time
I could think

in fact, for George getting nervous
made it worse for him
the small cells spread everywhere in the brain

I'm like an alcoholic
George would say
the funny part
when you consider it
is that I don't even need a drink to get drunk

I feel dizzy all the time
I have to lie down
Liz, is that you
why did you change your hair

I was not going to answer
George was trying to provoke me
that would start a strange discussion
about what is a reality
and the cost of hairdressing
George was still trying to manage
to spend his money skilfully

and me
cooking, cooking all the time
not being able to do anything else
because George's taste was continuously changing
I hate potatoes
you are always making French fries

I thought
is this a symptom
or is this the man I love
life can be so strange
what you think you know, you don't
and what you think you don't, you know
like the temperature in Maine
along the sea

so, please, let's skip that part
I don't want you to see him
the way he was in his last days
George was so proud of himself
well, everything I own is yours, Liz

you're rich now
I gave you all I have

oh, George, don't talk about that

I love you with your present
your past and your future

George, you're so nice

I would soon discover
what he meant by those words

CHAPTER ELEVEN
I Can Feel It!

You came here with someone else

no

don't say no, Liz
I can feel it
you were here with him

it was such a long time ago

yes, but you did

yes

you just said no

I didn't recognize the place

and now you do

it has changed a lot
this house was not a condo at that time
it was a big summer cottage
no insulation
maybe a three-season house
everything has changed
I met you
and my whole life was different

but you came here before
don't deny it

yes, I did

I was right

it's the ocean, George
everybody likes the ocean

I was so right
I could not stop having those strange feelings
and the way you act, Liz
always looking back
are you afraid your lover would be right behind you

George, come on
it was such a long time ago
nothing is the same anymore
I fell in love with you

but that was in the city
we met in the city
you always wanted me to settle at the beach
I know why, now
what was his name already
Paul, Bob, Arthur, the one you call Art in your sleep

stop it, George
stop bitching at me

or a plain John
John Doe would be enough
a stranger in my life
in our life, ah

George, you're not funny

so there you are
you came here with him
maybe you would just sit on the porch
or in front of the cottage
watching the waves
hiding from the sun
in his arms
maybe you were freezing
it could have been one of those days
and you'd ask him for his coat
no, don't answer
don't tell me
let me guess
I can see you
I can see both of you
there's not even a cloud in the sky
not a chance of rain
thunderstorms would have been ok with me
nothing but a hot August sunny day
the water
how wonderful during that time of the year
was cool
not icy
just cool
and the beach was not too crowded

George, why don't you just relax
this was such a long time ago
it was written in the stars
that I had to know this place
before I knew you

shut up, Liz
I don't want to hear any more from you
you came here before

he is dead now

I saw a picture of you on Facebook
I am sure it was taken by him

oh, George
it was taken maybe thirty years ago
Sam put it in my album
she thought it would be nice
to look at her mother the way she was
when she was young

I knew it
he took the picture

I didn't say that

it's all the same

I know the drill, George
anything you say can be
and will be used against you

I don't want to hear you anymore
you came here before
with someone else
that's enough
I don't want any details

I'm sorry, George
I am so sorry
but at that time
I haven't even met you
you were not yet a part of my life
it was such a long time ago
and, and, and
the poor fellow died in a car accident
two weeks after the picture was taken

if not, you'd be with him today
don't tell me I'm wrong
I know it

I am with you, George
I have always been with you

the guy is dead
and I can feel his ghost
wandering around this place
I can see his ghost right behind you
when I look at you under the sun
I can feel he is all around you

I can feel he loves you
more than I do
and he is the one
who makes me sick

CHAPTER TWELVE
Steve Birdsky Is Dead!

When you sell life insurance
you must expect that one day or another
one of your clients will die

I knew that
but I thought I would be lucky
in a sense
well, you know
that I would die before any one of them did

I selected them
I made sure to reject the boozers, the fatsos
the drunk drivers
I have been doing that for forty years

can you imagine
tossing a coin in the air
without ever
getting the other side of the coin
heads or tails
it never missed
I began to think
I was flipping a two-headed coin
that I was lucky enough to find one
or even luckier than that
I was convinced at one point
that it was the coin that has found
its way to me trough all my life

nobody is immortal

I used to say that
it was a part of my sales pitch
they listened
it worked
on others
it didn't work on me
maybe because I was saying it so often
it didn't sound real to me

Steve Birdsky had a family
two kids, a wife
a dog and a cat, for God's sake
why do poor people spend money on dogs
they eat so much
it was a big dog
a St. Bernard

I kept asking myself
time after time
for no reason
just looking at him
and considering how skinny he was
his eyes
would fill with tears for no apparent reason
the way he would breathe
and the dog
the poor thing
a very passive animal
not normal for a pet
not even wagging his tail
I used to look at both of them

it was a strange sight
a man and a dog
both being old
sick
you might say
both with gray hair
and surviving that kind of way
they had nothing to loose
looking at each other
as if
one was already gone, disappeared
maybe it was the cataract

I should have known better
forced him out of my business
got rid of him as a client
but he used to pay well
cash and carry
that was my saying about him

he had a life
like you and me
a house, a car

how will they manage without him

why are you looking at me this strange way, Liz

they were insured, weren't they
and, above all, by you
George
the most respected broker in town

yes and no
that is the problem, Liz
how do you think we could afford
the downpayment on the cottage
two hundred grand
that was a lot of money at the time
I had to be a swift operator

it was cheaper for those who paid in cash
they'd get a receipt
that's all
I kept the money
I was selling wind, don't you understand

as long as they were alive

George kept on talking and talking
I think it was the pills
I was getting used to his strange ways recently

I was not listening, really

on TV, there was an ad
we could see a guy
a big strong guy
so big
he must have weighted five times
the weight of a normal person
he was dressed as a sumo wrestler
slanted eyes drawn with makeup
and talking silly

he was dropping down on the couch
almost falling
worse even
throwing himself in the air
and landing right on the couch
an old couch
and that was the punchline
an old couch reinforced with plastic shingles
he was doing that to show the resistance
of it

it was so solid
and it was so cheap

$29.99
twenty-nine ninety-nine
a voice was shouting the price
with a false Japanese accent
so false it sounded funny

I was under the impression
the ad was running in a loop
the guy, the sumo guy
weighing more than 500 pounds
would you believe
George, you're not listening
falling, falling again
on the poor couch

George, we should buy
something like that
before it is too late
our couch will soon fall apart

just call now
only $29.99
over and over

we will buy one
and you will get better, George
and we will save the expense of a new couch

Liz, Liz
don't you understand
Steve Birdsky is dead
staying alive
is not an option
for me
anymore

Steve Birdsky is dead
and I am dead along with him
dead broke

Other Books by the Author

La Cadillac du docteur Watson, Lévesque éditeur, 2013
Celle d'avant, celle d'après, Lévesque éditeur, 2012
Buddha Airlines, Les herbes rouges, 2009
La séparation, Les herbes rouges, 2007
La bibliothèque de Sodome, Les herbes rouges, 2008
La manufacture de machines, XYZ éditeur, 2001
Manuscrit trouvé dans une valise, Éditions Quinze, 1979
Récits des temps ordinaires, Éditions du Jour, 1972
Je suis un chien, Éditions de La Grenouillère, 2013
Textes d'accompagnement, L'Aurore, 1975
Textes extraits de vanille, L'Aurore, 1974
Le cinéma de Petite-Rivière, Éditions du Jour, 1974
Le Roi Jaune, Éditions du Jour, 1971
Monsieur Blacquières, Éditions de La Grenouillère, 2014
Vieillir, Les herbes rouges, 2011
Les poèmes d'amour, Les herbes rouges, 2010
La chute de l'ange, Les herbes rouges, 2009
Correspondance de guerre, Les herbes rouges, 2008
Le livre des plages, Les herbes rouges, 2007
Le petit catéchisme, Éditions de l'Hexagone, 1972
Les mangeurs de terre, Éditions du Jour, 1970
Les épisodes de l'oeil, Éditions de l'Estérel, 1967